NUMBER ONE

Essays on the American West
sponsored by the
Elma Dill Russell Spencer Foundation

Aspects of the American West
THREE ESSAYS

Aspects of the American West

THREE ESSAYS BY
Joe B. Frantz

Foreword by W. Eugene Hollon

TEXAS A&M UNIVERSITY PRESS
College Station and London

Copyright © 1976 by Joe B. Frantz

Library of Congress Cataloging in Publication Data
Aspects of the American West.

(Essays on the American West; no. 1)
"Sponsored by the Elma Dill Russell Spencer Foundation."

Includes bibliographical references.

Contents: Yellowstone National Park.—Western impact on the Nation.—The American West: child of Federal subsidy.

1. Yellowstone National Park—Addresses, essays, lectures. 2. The West—History—Addresses, essays, lectures. 3. Government spending policy—The West—Addresses, essays, lectures. I. Elma Dill Russell Spencer Foundation. II. Title. III. Series.

F722.F75   978   76-17973
ISBN 0-89096-023-2

To
Walter Prescott Webb
who first faced me westward

Contents

Foreword

WHEN Frank Wardlaw asked if I would write a brief introduction to a series of essays by my good friend Joe B. Frantz, the opportunity proved irresistible. Frank assured me that a Xerox copy of the manuscript "would be arriving from Joe within the next three or four days." But knowing the author so well and so long, I had no illusion that he would ever violate a principle and meet a deadline. Surely enough, eighty-three days passed before the package arrived, along with the following note from the publisher: "Here at long last they are—three essays that are vintage Frantz. I think that they will make a fine little book. Be as insulting as you like."

That last sentence reflects upon a relationship of more than thirty years that has been almost as close as that which existed between Lewis and Clark. It has tied the bonds of friendship so securely that Joe and I take delight in insulting one another publicly on particular occasions. At the same time, we have shared some memorable moments over the years. I remember a particular night in Oklahoma a long time ago when we stood at the large window of our living room and witnessed the most terrifying electrical storm imaginable—

fearful that the next bolt of lightning would strike us dead. Then there was a much quieter experience in Maine when the two of us sat on a ledge extending out over the water early one morning and watched a heavy fog roll in from the ocean and listened to the incoming tide slam against the rocky coast. For almost an hour we were hypnotized by the sights and sounds of the Atlantic, completely oblivious that anything else of importance was going on in the outside world.

We have participated in historical sessions at national conventions dozens of times since our first joint appearance in 1946. Sometimes we have read companion papers of a so-called scholarly nature. On other occasions, one has served as chairman of the session and introduced the other, or vice versa. As a master of the "quick comeback," Joe is very difficult indeed to beat in a game of matching wits.

While introducing him at the Western Historical meeting in Omaha, Nebraska, when he presented the essay entitled "Western Impact on the Nation," I compared his presence to that of "a fresh breeze over a Texas outhouse." The phrase brought a spontaneous response from the large audience, but Joe was more than equal to the occasion, and his ad lib remarks proved my point perfectly. On a similar occasion at a historical meeting in Dallas, one of the participants in the session later approached me in a very confidential manner. "What is this feud between you and Joe Frantz all about? You fellows seem to despise one another."

"Ted, you obviously don't understand us Texans very well," I replied. "When we are as close as Joe and I, anything goes. It's all part of the Texas spirit, if you want to call it that, or in keeping with our traditional frontier sense of humor. Now, if Joe and I hated each other's guts, as Texans are very capable of doing at times, we would either ignore one another completely or else affect overpoliteness."

Many people have asked if there really *is* a Joe B. Frantz. I first heard about him soon after World War II, when Dr. Walter Prescott Webb mentioned casually that "We have a young man who is back from the navy and is writing a biography of Gail Borden. I think that his forthcoming dissertation will be one of the best ever turned out by the Department of History at the University of Texas." I mentioned the comment a few days later to Savoie Lottinville, then director of the University of Oklahoma Press. Savoie expressed an immediate interest in the manuscript, and I forgot all about the matter until an announcement by the press appeared a year or so later about a forthcoming book entitled *Gail Borden: Dairyman to a Nation,* by one Joe B. Frantz. The book won the prestigious Carr P. Collins Award of the Texas Institute of Letters in 1951 and Joe was on his way. My claiming credit sometimes for the publication of Frantz's first book doubtless is undeserved, but it furnishes an excellent excuse to remind him now and then about his many obligations to me.

To thousands of scholars and people in general, Joe B. Frantz *is* the Department of History at the University of Texas, perhaps to the chagrin of some of his colleagues with Ivy League credentials who pretend that the real history of this country stopped at the Mississippi River. Even so, Joe is extremely visible (in spite of what some would argue to the contrary) and has a host of friends and acquaintances in every state in the Union, plus several foreign countries. At times it is exasperatingly difficult to locate him, and a call to his office usually results in an explanation by a long-suffering secretary that "Dr. Frantz will not return from Washington until next Monday." If not Washington, it is just as apt to be Lima, Peru; Logan, Utah; or even Kerrville, Texas.

Professor Jim Pearson tells the story of overhearing two graduate students on the Austin campus one day. "There goes Dr. Joe B. Frantz," the first one said, "I have a class with him this semester." His companion pointed out that the particular individual was somebody else and not Dr. Frantz. When the first student insisted that he was correct, the other one finally observed, "Man, don't you know that Joe B. Frantz is just a figment of the administration's imagination?"

If the author of the present essays remains eternally overcommitted to publishers, invariably late for appointments, or off on another "flying trip" to God-knows-where, it is primarily because he considers time as an illusionary tyranny that should be either abolished or ignored. Once he is "cornered" by a friend or even a perfect stranger, he is good for at least thirty minutes of humorous or serious conversation, or a mixture of both. Every "visiting fireman" drops in at his office for a visit. As a result, Joe finds that he frequently has to get out of town in order to get some writing done. Once he starts, he can turn out a superbly written book or essay in record time. Few can match his ability to reduce complex substance to understandable English, and fewer yet have a more imaginative mind for a proper word or phrase. In brief, Joe has the rare ability to take ordinary day-to-day happenings and fit the bits and pieces into a larger mosaic of meaningful history. His well-deserved reputation as a raconteur is matched by a perceptive intellect and a great sense of timing.

The man's writing style is as original and free as his spirit. Who else could paint a more imaginative word portrait as a self-made Westerner proclaiming the virtues of free enterprise: "When that long-legged son-of-a-gun stands up in a cattleman's club in Cheyenne, or in a chamber of commerce banquet in Tucson, or at a governors' conference in Helena, and when he issues a blast at an all-consuming federal encroachment in words more blistering than all the winds that blow from Spokane to San Antonio, is he historically sound, or has he swallowed a whole hunk of home-manufactured, self-illuminated halo without chewing it first?"

Few individuals are born with a natural talent for writing. For most it remains a painful struggle to avoid overuse of passive verbs, trite alliterations, misplaced commas, and overworked cliches. My best instructors have been copy editors of various publishing houses, combined with a "brass posterior." Consequently, I have tried to pass on to my graduate students certain points about paragraph construction that every author learns from experience. Then, along comes a man like Joe Frantz who violates everything I have preached against for decades—not to mention every rule in a publisher's manual of style. Joe's sentences (more often non-sentences) can give a high school teacher apoplexy. Yet, who would be foolish enough to tamper with a unique, pithy style that has become his trademark? Certainly not me!

Like most liberal, intellectual Texans, Frantz has long carried on a love-hate relationship with his native state. Although he can be devastatingly critical of the army of home-grown political clowns, self-made millionaires who flaunt their wealth and equate capitalism with Christianity, and Neanderthal newspaper editors, he has little patience with those who feel compelled to depreciate anything and everything that carries a Texas brand.

I was fortunate to be there when Joe presented his essays "Child of Federal Subsidy" and "Western Impact on the Nation" to audiences of professional historians. Reading them after a lapse of several years has been a refreshing experience. The article relating to the Yellowstone National Park was previously unknown to me, but it represents the author's catholic interest and broad knowledge and appreciation of the American West. Meanwhile, "Child of Federal Subsidy" attracted more attention than any single essay that Joe ever delivered. He read it at the annual meeting of the American Historical Association in Philadelphia on December 28, 1963, five weeks after President Kennedy's assassination in Dallas. The wire services picked it up, and newspaper and magazine editors throughout the country gave the author and the article national exposure.

The many close friends who carry on a regular correspondence with Joe Frantz long ago recognized that he has used letter writing as a special art form. The following paragraph, selected at random from a very thick personal file, reveals as much about the man as the total contents of this introduction. It is typical of what Frank Wardlaw called "vintage Frantz": "I am at my office on a Sunday trying to catch up on some of my back correspondence. The clouds outside are lowering, a cold front heads this way. We might get a rain, though I don't know whether I would recognize one if I saw it. The thing I like about this weather is that Helen has laid out a regimen of yard work for me, but I contended that it was going to rain too hard to get into it. For once, I won."

Toledo, Ohio   W. Eugene Hollon

Aspects of the American West
THREE ESSAYS

Yellowstone National Park: Genesis of an Urban Solution

I<small>F</small> I were a dramatist like William Shakespeare, Eugene O'Neill, Tennessee Williams, or your Uncle Eddie, who writes Easter pageants for the local cell of the Eastern Star, I would divide this morality play into two acts. Act One would be historical, and deal with Then. Act Two would be analytical, and deal with Now. So let's raise the curtain on Then, and see how it all got started.

In the white man's world, awareness of Yellowstone goes back at least to when the French fur trappers learned to talk with Indians along the upper Missouri and its tributaries. The first American actually to see the grandeur of Yellowstone was John Colter, who had left the Lewis and Clark expedition on its return trip to go trapping on his own. Although a modest man with a reputation for veracity, Colter met only disbelief when he returned to civilization to relate what he had seen.

Delivered as "The Meaning of Yellowstone," Norman Furniss Lecture at Colorado State University, Fort Collins, Feb. 9, 1972, and subsequently published in *Montana: The Magazine of Western History* 22, no. 3 (Sept., 1972): 5–11.

Over the next six decades Colter's experience was repeated periodically as lone explorers adventured into the Yellowstone country and then returned to settlements to regale skeptics with accounts of the wonders they had witnessed: tinted valleys and towering waterfalls and profound lakes and, most of all, a festering earth spewing hot brimstone from a pocked face full of seemingly endless open sores. Jim Bridger, equally redoubtable as a mountain man and windbag, met the same scant acceptance when he related the strangeness of this country bordering the Yellowstone River.

Finally, of course, enough reports came in that like the sightings of unidentified flying objects their credibility had to be investigated, if for no other reason than to shut off the sense of wonder. Was there really such a back door to hell, or did something about the wilderness unravel men's normal chain of logic and memory? The federal government resolved to find out for sure.

Thus, in 1870 the Washburn-Langford-Doane expedition of nineteen men visited Yellowstone under military auspices to see whether Jim Bridger really had been telling the truth when he amused auditors in Virginia City with his vivid description of a body of water as thick as a man shooting into the air from a hole in the ground and climbing upward until it reached the height of the town flagpole. The only reason anyone in that Montana metropolis halfway believed Jim was that he kept the height of the steaming column within reason instead of claiming that it spouted a thousand or more feet. The expedition found that, if anything, Bridger had understated the glories of Yellowstone.

One September night, when the Washburn expedition was preparing to leave Yellowstone, its members sat around their after-supper campfire comparing notes on what each had seen. They were sufficiently material-minded to see the enormous tourist potentialities of the region. What would be the best speculative approach? they pondered. In the deepening evening one of the party, Cornelius Hedges, observed that reaping private profit for a public miracle was not right and should not be permitted. Instead, he argued, what they had seen should be taken over by the federal government and preserved for all of the people of the United States. Hedges hit a sensitive chord, and the campers agreed that each would push toward such a project.

On their return to Helena, reports were filed, appropriate congressmen were pressured, and soon a real movement to preserve Yellowstone in its virginal state was under way. Langford was the prime motivator and over the following winter made vigorous speeches in such distant centers of influence as Washington, New York, and Minneapolis. The *New York Tribune* of January 23, 1871, quoted him as saying that while the United States already had Niagara and Yosemite, "This is probably the most remarkable region of natural attractions in the world; . . . this new field of wonders should be at once withdrawn from occupancy, and set apart as a public National Park for the enjoyment of the American people for all time."

Moving with a celerity hardly duplicable today, a bill was introduced in Congress the following December and was endorsed by the secretary of the interior on January 29; photographs taken by the subsequent Hayden expedition were laid before almost every member of Congress, thereby convincing the unconvinced; Langford's publications in *Scribner's* were likewise distributed; the brass from Montana was forever buttonholing; and, when the vote was taken, the Senate had one dissenter—from California—while the House count was two to one in favor. On March 1, 1872, President U. S. Grant signed the bill.

One hundred years ago, then, the government of the United States authorized the first national park in the world. It was virtually inaccessible to the people for whom it was being saved, and many thought with justification that it would be impossible for western soldiers to guard, but it was there, secure for the ages, its only long-range problem stemming from the multiplication and mobility of the masses unborn who formed its future clients.

Yellowstone, far and away America's favorite natural public lure (no work of God can compete with man-made Disneyland East or West, evidently), has since become the mother of more than twelve hundred parks and preserves scattered over almost one hundred nations. Important as Yellowstone is in its own right, its greater importance lies in its establishment of a principle that has spread throughout the world. When on March 1, 1872, Congress set Yellowstone apart "as a public park or pleasuring ground for the benefit and enjoyment of the people," it unwittingly implanted the idea that man must retain sanctuaries, places of preferably quiet retreat where he can see what the land was like in its original intentions before man, the upright and thinking animal, could intrude his presence thereon. Somewhere man must encounter space on earth and renew his opportunity to know the spell of silence and to contemplate the sorcery of natural wonders, both seen and unseen.

For what scant comfort one can draw amidst present budget stringencies, Congress dallied more than six years before making its first appropriation for Yellowstone, finally coming through in the summer of 1878 with a ten-thousand-dollar appropriation for the management and development of an almost inaccessible wilderness the size of Connecticut. During that period the first superintendent, N. P. Langford, managed Yellowstone without salary, a service for which he deserves to be made the fifth at Mount Rushmore.

Of course, the public park concept was not new, either in this country or abroad. At its inception Washington, D.C., itself was envisioned as a rotary park-capital. Frederick Law Olmsted, revered for many accomplishments, is most appreciated for setting aside that green belt in the middle of Manhattan Island which we know as Central Park and which we also know could not be afforded today on Lindsay's, Beame's, or anyone else's budget. In California, almost a decade before Yellowstone, Yosemite had been considered sufficiently worthy that the federal government had directed California to withdraw it as a state preserve from private exploitation, thereby unwittingly freezing Yosemite for future absorption almost three decades later into the federal government's developing park system.

But Yellowstone the park and Yellowstone the idea came first as national concerns, and as the world compresses and crowds, the precepts of both teach and preach more forcefully a century later than they did during that uncertain beginning. Yellowstone has become more than a place to see and sense. It is a world-wide symbol, a flaming evangelist to those who believe remembrance of some things past is necessary for sanity in a mad present and for assurance that there will be a future founded on more than statistical ciphers.

But man, however grand around a campfire, is also petty and angling at work. Naturally enough, with interdepartmental jealousy being a cornerstone of any public policy, Yellowstone became embroiled immediately in a fight for the right to administer between the army, which generally superintended the West, and the Department of the Interior, young and on the make. Probably Mr. Gallup would have found that more Americans preferred control by the army, whose heroes had just been knighted barely half a decade before for saving the Union, over Interior, an upstart, full of aggressive civilians with theoretical approaches to the real problems of anything. In the case of Yellowstone, the country needed roads, removal of the Indian threat, and settlers. The army knew how to run the West and to provide these services. On the other hand, Interior was a nest of idealists, some of whom might even tell you that people should be herded into the corner and pockets of Yellowstone instead of turning the park over to builders and developers.

Except in detail, the fight between the army and Interior sounds remarkably like the *sub rosa* sniping that goes on right now between the theoreticians and the pragmatists in both Interior and the Corps of Engineers, as in today's running fight in the Everglades.

Regardless of intragovernment jousting, Yellowstone started something. In the decades ahead, other park areas were set aside for the pleasure of the public until thirteen parks and eighteen national monuments had been created by acts of Congress, necessitating the establishment of some formal administrative agency, which, after the usual jockeying and power plays, if I may mix sports, became the National Park Service in 1916. As every student of lower-division American history surveys knows, the demand for conservation was growing, for three-fourths of our original forestland had been denuded, rivers permitted to silt up, grass grazed off, and once fallow land rendered unfit. A Forest Service had been created in 1905. And, because of an assassin's hand, Theodore Roosevelt, that most vocal champion of sound conservation, had become president in 1901.

Roosevelt, never modest, has received his share of the credit for making protection of natural resources respectable and popular. His activities in the cause were varied, ranging from reclamation to propaganda. Most notable among Rooseveltian procedures was the Conservation Conference of Governors, which he called and supervised in 1908. It brought together the nation's names and intellects, including, of course, the governors of the states. Although not much was said about national parks, everyone went home baptized in the waters of conservation and inspired by the messianic fervor of the president himself.

Meanwhile, the increase in numbers of national parks was slow. Despite the early implicit approval of Yosemite, Yellowstone National Park was nearly two decades old before that California combination of craggy tumult and meadowed serenity was brought under federal control. At the same time, California received two other national parks, Sequoia and tiny General Grant, long since absorbed into King's Canyon. Far to the east in Arkansas a section and a half surrounding an area of smelly hot springs was set aside for its curative as well as its curious qualities. Slowly, other additions were made—Crater Lake, gigantic Glacier, Colorado's Mesa Verde, Mount Rainier—altogether more than nine million acres of scenic wonders to be administered without any real systematization. The General Land Office, the Department of the Interior, the War Department, with its guardianship necessities, and the Department of Agriculture all had a hand in running one or more parks. Besides these, five national military parks, all Civil War battlefields, were managed by the War Department, which was also responsible for road building in Yellowstone and Crater Lake. Notably, except for the battlefields, none of the parks and monuments lay east of Arkansas. In fact, except for Platt in Oklahoma and Hot Springs, all lay west, usually well west, of the hundredth meridian in the country where, as football coaches would say, the real West with its real scenery really begins. In size, the tracts ranged from Platt with its 912 acres to Yellowstone with its more than 2 million acres. Under this haphazard supervisory pattern, precise criteria were unknown and probably impossible.

But every addition had one thing in common. Each had entered the federal preserve over the opposition of local private interests, which had coveted timber, pasture, mineral rights, or water. Opposition had intensified in direct proportion to the immediate speculative hopes of the potential exploiters. Every withdrawal represented a victory for the common people over the private developer.

Eventually, even Congress acceded to the necessities for organization. Theodore Roosevelt had believed in a national park system. William Howard Taft with his more orderly outlook had been explicit in his recommendations. Finally, the 62d Congress in 1912 and its successor in 1913 had seen bills introduced, neither of which advanced as far as a committee report. But with the convening of the 64th Congress on the first Monday of December, 1915, young Democratic Congressman John E. Raker, whose district included Yosemite and who was father of the two previous abortive bills, again introduced his national park bill. For strategic purposes a second bill was shortly introduced by another California congressman, William Kent, a Republican turned Progressive turned independent. Both bills went to committee, which then issued a rewritten bill with Kent as designated sponsor. Despite strong opposition, the bill passed the House, and in the Senate it picked up a champion in Reed Smoot of Utah and high tariff fame. On August 25, 1916, authorization for the National Park Service as a bureau within the Department of the Interior received President Wilson's signature. Forty-five years after the first national park was authorized, a system for managing Yellowstone and its descendant parks had finally been created. No longer would the chaotic situation described by the biographer of the first director of the National Park Service, Steve Mather, be in force:

[29]

In Yellowstone, all improvements and their appropriations were managed by an officer of the Army Corps of Engineers, who answered to neither the Interior Department nor the park superintendent; the superintendent was himself an Army officer, appointed by the Secretary of War; and "exclusive control" rested with the Secretary of the Interior. Crater Lake and Mt. Rainier, like Yellowstone, used Army engineers for road-building and improvements, and in those two parks the superintendent was a civilian, appointed by the Secretary of the Interior. On the other hand, Yosemite, Sequoia, and General Grant had Army superintendents but no Army engineers.[1]

Besides that, the West, where the parks and monuments were located, had moved beyond its Old West psychosis and purpose. No Indians were likely to make forays into the parks, Anglo and other holdouts against federal order had been subdued by time and termination of their mortality, and soldiers were no longer needed. Was it a proper military occupation to prevent forest fires, explain the slow growth of redwoods to tourists, and rescue those hapless, innocent drivers of 1910 cars who got stuck in sand or ran out of water? With the secretary of the interior always at his elbow urging that the soldiers be pulled out, the secretary of war saw that the time had come to give the wonders of this world into the tenderer hands of the civilians. Congress and President Wilson had recognized that the nation had enough federal parks to deserve a system, and the National Park Service was in business.

End of Act One.

[1] Robert Shankland, *Steve Mather of the National Parks*, 3d ed. (New York: Alfred A. Knopf, 1970), p. 104.

In musical terms the first act would be marked an-dante. Now we move into a cacophony designated scherz-ando, allegretto, frisky, and acid rock.

Act Two's curtain rises with the mist in Acadia Na-tional Park in Maine. Acadia is open the year around, but only for three months between Memorial Day and Labor Day is anyone there. Then it becomes a Summer Place, a Summer of '42, a place in which things happen. It is a jewel of a park, small by western standards, fragile. Yet in those three intense months nearly one and three-quarters million people pour through Acadia. It has one lookout point, Cadillac Mountain, a mere hillock by Rocky Mountain standards, but on a crisp June day the parked cars are backed down it until they create a traffic hazard practically all the way back into Bar Harbor's lobster pens. If Cadillac's summit over-looked Los Angeles, the great outdoorsmen there would finish its leveling and then pave it, unless they could find some place to hang a house over its side. But since Cadil-lac is made of hard New England rock, California de-velopers would find it a dull place to build, with scant chance of its sliding into the valley the next time the rain shifted its undergirding of mud. (For stage direc-tions our pit orchestra should now strike up "How Firm a Foundation.")

The attraction of Acadia is partially that it's ex-quisite and partially that it's there. It has trails that are easy to walk, it is ten minutes from town, and it has rocks and vistas of deep blue bays, plus sailboats to watch. It is no place to back-pack or to camp. Come out in the morning, go in for lunch, come back in the late evening, and watch scattered lights awake on the dark green islands dotted about like beckoning sentinels. In the evening when most of the cars go home, Acadia is large enough to get out of this world in.

Its superintendent, a thoughtful, poetic man, is talking: "If the crowds keep coming, I don't see how we can survive. We have Central Park traffic in an idyllic setting. The people are ruining the park, yet the park exists for the people.

"We know that in corners of the park parties are held of which we cannot approve. But how far do you police against people who are enjoying themselves without hurting anyone? The meanest groups which we've encountered are those on a beer bust, which is basically inside the law. So many of the parties that we know take place, though outside legal sanction, are quiet private affairs, but one of our functions is to uphold the law in the parks. Do you ignore a bunch of noisy, belligerent beer drinkers, spoiling for a nasty fight? At the same time, do you bust another group that just wants to do its thing on its own bare boulder, only because your sense of smell tells you they're breaking the law? How much are we policemen? How much preservationists and interpreters, helping people to see and feel with sensitivity?"

Quick curtain. The scene rises in the South, a land traditionally reminiscent of redolent magnolias and languorous belles and field hands singing softly above a banjo's plucking, not to mention hookworm, ringworm, malaria, fat-fried food, illiteracy, and mean-eyed men with murder in their hearts on Saturday and the fundamentals of the faith in their pious souls the next morning. Here Tennessee and North Carolina share the Smokies as the southernmost extension of a string of pearls of parks that stretch from Shenandoah down the Blue Ridge Parkway almost from Washington, D.C., to Atlanta. In the South the Great Smoky Mountain National Park is the queen of them all, a brooding mother wilderness right out of colonial days, with even a Cade's Cove where the old farmer will grind your cornmeal with a waterwheel and a mule or jackass will walk around and around until you get old-fashioned sorghum. The Smokies take you back, transport you out of this raucous world into an encounter with enchantment with simple wonders. You half expect to run onto Davy Crockett or Daniel Boone, long rifles over buckskin-covered shoulders.

You need this feeling, for you likely have come to the Smokies through its greedy greeting sister, the town of Gatlinburg. Gatlinburg, Tennessee, is as tawdry and synthetic and commercial as anything you would see in Las Vegas, Virginia City, West Yellowstone, Gettysburg, or a slum in San Juan, where the worst section is ironically called *la perla*, "the pearl." Gatlinburg has wax museums, neon-lighted crosses and an every-evening reenactment of Calvary, cheap souvenirs by the millions, and traffic that would rival that of Paris or Rome. To go through Gatlinburg to get to the Smokies is a shattering experience, and practically no one can stay long enough in that mountain island to recover from getting there. And if he does, he has got to go back, or go out through Asheville, which is an improvement only because it has more than one street. The impression of greater Asheville is that of torn-up roads, groaning bulldozers, religious encampments with made-up names like Junalaska, and signboards by the fistful.

Let's try Texas. The Big Bend is better, in that it's the devil to get into and frequently the devil to endure. Basically it is wild country, and the nearest town of any size, one hundred miles away, is Alpine, not exactly everyone's dream of a second home.[2] Here's an isolated principality that competes with Yellowstone in size and exceeds it in remoteness. And only a comparative handful of people visit it each year.

And how do people react to this opportunity really to get away from it all? They wind into Big Bend's Chisos Basin, where the concessions are, and usually that's where they stay. Except for the very hardy, they watch the sunset, listen to a naturalist talk, hire a horse for a short ride to the Rim, where they can say they've "seen" Mexico, and complain because there's nothing to do. What really galls them is that since Big Bend is two hundred miles to anywhere, and the basin is ringed by mountains, TV is out, a fact with which they can live, but worse, they are denied effective use of their transistors. As long as you are in the Big Bend, you have to live without the Dow Jones averages, the results of the Denver Broncos *versus* the San Diego Chargers, the peregrinations of the president of the United States, the latest conjecturings on whether there really was a Howard Hughes, and Don McLean chanting his "American Pie" for eight straight minutes. So many people have

2 H. Allen Smith, the late humorist-author of *Low Man on a Totem Pole*, *Rhubarb*, and a basket of other books, decided that Alpine would make an ideal retirement home. The story of his subsequent feud with the townspeople ranks somewhere between hilarious and dreadful.

lamented that the Big Bend is dull. It's even worse for the kids, because there are no playgrounds, no swings, no swimming pools, no bicycles, just that one horseback ride which takes too much time if you're going to make El Paso before dark.

On to Mesa Verde, a fantastic window looking out on a long-gone American past. A summer-crowded park, yes, but with enough room that one can live with it. And then you go into the concession shops. Greasy napkins, messy skeins of spilled mustard on the floor, the out-of-doors, spring-fresh smell of yesterday's fried grease. And worse, because they don't go away with cleaning, the souvenir counters. To be charitable, so much of what is sold is junk made in Japan or Hong Kong or Dallas, whereas within reach is an Indian culture with traditions of centuries of native art. Navajo blankets and rugs are expensive, and the concessionaire explains that visitors want dollar items to take back to the boys at the office, or for the kiddies to remind them that they have been there or just to silence them cheaply. All right, so you can't afford a rug. Colorado is one rocky state, and as just one possibility, key rings fashioned with polished stones can be produced in quantity and sold cheaply. They would speak of Colorado and Mesa Verde considerably more eloquently than those postcards with leering lines and pillows that not even a tsetse fly could appreciate.

And now we're in Yosemite. A little boy is crying. He has a pain in his middle, or a badly cut knee. His slightly older brother is playing nurse and Oral Roberts, and the concerned ranger is asking him where his parents are. "In Las Vegas," he sobs. Or Los Angeles, or

San Francisco. The parents have driven to the park, aware that in the campgrounds tents are practically stake-to-stake. They have set up junior and sub-junior, stacked enough groceries to last them for a week, made sure that the transistor works, and admonished them to look for a ranger in case anything goes wrong. Without knowing it, the National Park Service has suddenly become a baby-sitter for parents who understandably want a vacation but either cannot or will not pay for someone to keep the children.

And then we're in Glacier, again remote and spacious. A few bears have still not been run off from Glacier, but they likely will go, and another fragment of America's natural past will have been lost. But now Mother is coaxing the bear into a position where she can put Baby's legs astraddle the animal's neck, meanwhile urging Daddy to take that picture quick. At the same time she is putting honey on the child's face so that the bear will lick it. Next fall the father will be the bore of the neighborhood as he shows how mother and child charmed the wild beast. Fine, fine, except that bears are fractious fellows with a low point of irritability. If the bear decides he wants more than he's getting, there's a mangled child or adult, and someone has gotten his name in the papers without being around to enjoy it. And from the jaws-of-death surroundings of his air-conditioned office, some journalist or talk-show pathfinder will spellbind an audience about the brutal perils of our national parks and the contempt of its personnel toward Mr. and Mrs. People and their safety.

And finally we pass that "mighty scarp of the

Tetons" to come home to Yellowstone. The first prodigy of the park world. Through it runs a federal highway, not as busy the year around as that one which connects Knoxville with Asheville, but in July in Yellowstone the traffic stacks up from here to as far as you can see. Yellowstone has always been famed for its amplitude, but for the basic three months of summer its traffic is bumper-to-bumper, and the man behind the man behind still another man eats gasoline fumes and exercises by slamming on brakes and fighting for hamburgers at a concession stand. This is a park experience? This is serenity? The only difference between driving in Yellowstone in summer and driving on the Los Angeles freeway is that in Los Angeles you can get lost more easily and quickly.

So the parks are packed, and the approaches are tasteless and gouging, and the concessionaires undiscriminating. Do we seal off the parks, as the purists, the Sierra Club types, insist? Do we save them for the few, the elite who can walk and pack? And in an increasingly urbanized situation in which ghetto dwellers are screaming with tension, what good is Yellowstone or the Smokies to a man or boy who does not know how to get across town by bus, even if he could afford to?

The truth is that in this centennial age we have reached the time for reconsideration of parks and their purposes. We still need the wilderness experience, but it is not an experience in which everyone can hope to share or even want to share fully. Instead, present need is for gradations of wilderness experience, each geared to the individual's capacities and probabilities. Ours is now a city civilization, as we all know, and those cities are in a race with time, to borrow from a title.[3]

Then what is the role of parks today? The proper heritage of Yellowstone in these times is the preservation of that natural wonder known as man. The National Park Service perforce is increasingly city oriented, to the dismay of many traditionalists, especially outdoorsmen. But the child in the central city, without access to mountains and aspens, instead needs a park's program that will focus on his relationship to *his* total environment. The park service needs to be an activist in educational programs that will mesh closely with the schools in areas far away from organized park boundaries.

The first parks, as noted, lay in the West, where trees towered like cathedrals and mountains reached for infinity. By and large all secretaries of the interior came from the West as recently as Stewart Udall and Walter Hickel. Perhaps change of direction was unconsciously noted by President Nixon when he named a Marylander, Rogers Morton, as the latest secretary of the interior. On the other hand, this geographical shift can be overemphasized, for John F. Kennedy as a candidate in 1960 liked to remind his audiences from Billings to Bismarck that "the two Americans of this century who did more to develop the resources of the United States, to conserve them, and protect them for other generations, . . . Theodore Roosevelt and Franklin Roosevelt,"[4] were

[3] Jeanne R. Lowe, *Cities in a Race with Time* (New York: Random House, 1967).

[4] *The Speeches, Remarks, Press Conferences, and Statements of Senator John F. Kennedy, August 1 through November 7, 1960*, Final Report of the Committee on Commerce, United States Senate, *Freedom*

both from the East. But then, Iowan Hoover was the most western president we'd had till the 1960's. But back to the problem.

If a city dweller, child or adult, surrounded and plagued by ugliness and noise, cannot see Old Faithful or visit with an alligator in the Everglades, perhaps he can establish some identity with his past by looking at the tasteful sandstone monument to Cabrillo outside San Diego or by contemplating the towering horseshoe which opens the door to the West in Saint Louis.

Look briefly at what has already happened: Fire Island and Cape Cod national seashores to service the teeming millions in the New York–Boston orbit. Assateague for Washington and Baltimore. Indiana Dunes for greater Chicago. An Ozark scenic riverway or the Appalachian Trail. A wilderness site and a wild river system. Forty-six new areas added to the National Park System during the five years of Udall and Lyndon Johnson, and a growth in the area governed by the National Park Service of more than 40 percent since 1963. (By two men from the West, I might interject.) And this after Fred Seaton, secretary of the interior under Eisenhower, announced that everything had been taken into the park system that needed to be.

And now the two most ambitious projects of them all, still in the planning stage but with enough momentum and support that their completion is virtually assured: the Gateway National Park East for the Manhattan area and Gateway West for San Francisco's bay region, enriching the lives of more millions of all ages

of Communications, Part I (Washington: U.S. Government Printing Office, 1961) , p. 331.

than even a dozen Fillmores East and West could ever hope to attain. Gateway East, farther along, staggers with its scope, reaching from Long Island and Breezy Point to New Jersey and Sandy Hook, clearing out high-priced property, contemplating a nearly free busing and ferry service with monitors to see that the people who need open space the most but know least how to find it can somehow break out of their inner city canyons. If we are growing a walled-in mass of people, then we must utilize the long experience and the varied resources of the National Park Service to bring the parks to the people to give them, as Frederick Law Olmsted suggested to the California legislature away back in 1865, "The occasional contemplation of natural scenes of impressive character, . . . if this contemplation occurs in connection with relief from ordinary cares, change of air and change of habits, [it] is favorable to the health and vigor of men; and especially to the health and vigor of their intellect . . . it not only gives pleasure for the time being, but increases the subsequent capacity for happiness and the means of securing happiness."[5]

To try to intrude happiness into the beleaguered lives of huddled city dwellers, the National Park Service now manages more significant park land in and near large urban centers than any other agency of government at any level. Washington, D.C., with its peculiar problems, has living history and summer-in-the-parks programs that provide both education and recreation. They are all part of a new concept in the National Park

[5] Frederick Law Olmsted, "The Yosemite Valley and the Mariposa Big Trees: A Preliminary Report (1865)," *Landscape Architecture* 43 (Oct., 1952): 17.

Service—a concept of creativity and experimentation that also involves such existing institutions as schools and the Department of Housing and Urban Development. Buildings listed on the National Historic Register can no longer be bulldozed into oblivion until a thorough investigation by the National Park Service has proven that the building no longer speaks to the people who will see it. Wanton clearing of space for housing developments, supermarkets, and huge road and airport projects has been considerably diminished, although the battle is not over and the opposition is astute, aggressive, and persevering.

Meanwhile, the National Park Service is trying to get rid of its image as another impersonal agency in far-off Washington and instead is trying to work closely with all governments from local to national, inside and outside of this country. At one time or another park service experts are on leave in Nepal, Ethiopia, Japan—wherever a government is concerned with preserving and improving its natural areas and its historic places.

While this concern for bringing parks to the people is uppermost in the thinking of the bureau's leaders, the National Park Service thinking still does not believe that the special preserves were saved to be trampled. Impossible though it may be to draw hard and fast lines about how many people in a park are too many, the service is trying to weigh some kind of balance between numbers and needs. Like many an urban area, the service questions the sanctity of the automobile and doubts whether it is obligated to build a park road, a parking space, or trailer connections for every American who wishes to visit a park. Instead, park people are examining alternative means of transportation which will move more people into a park with less confusion and particularly with less strain on park resources. On the floor of Yosemite shuttle buses have already been tried, so that now the former harried father-driver can see the scenery instead of watching only for sudden stops by the car ahead. The new North Cascades and Guadalupe national parks will likely have roads only skirting one corner, and tramways will carry the people to the next most easily accessible spot. A tram or cable car can be installed without intruding too harshly on the scenery or disturbing much natural growth. If the tramway proves unsatisfactory, it can be removed, and only minimal scars will remain. But a road, almost any road, requires cutting and grading, which except for the more lush areas leaves an ugly gash in the countryside that will mar the beauty or the wildness of the scene, perhaps for generations. Besides, Yellowstone visitors should breathe something fresher than carbon monoxide.

Also, the park service has realized that today's people go to parks for vastly diverse purposes. The camper and the back-packer and the hiker like solitude. Some other families who might like such solitary activities can afford neither the time nor the expense. But are they not better off for a few hours' absence from the city than if they never came at all? Thus, the service plans for relatively easy access to the edges of parks, but feels no compulsion to build through or into the interior.

Further, campers today tend to divide into two groups, partially but not entirely segregated by age. One group likes to feel its experience during the daylight and turn in with the onset of night. To have another group night-partying, with music and laughter far past lights-out, is a jarring experience that ruins the whole adventure. So why not in places like Rocky Mountain National Park provide two campgrounds, one for day people and one for night people, sufficiently apart from each other that they won't disturb each other's inhabitants and sufficiently well marked that you will know which one to head for? If night merriment is your bag, then nothing in the rules of outdoor freedom, beyond common courtesy for sleeping neighbors, says your outdoor life-style shouldn't align itself with that of the owls. The park service is moving on the thesis that since everyone is people, people can gain from parks, whether they come to dream or to dance.

So here are our millions from the asphalt jungle daring to respond to the greenery of nearby parks or the amplitude of the West, the historic swamps of New Jersey or the interminable, eye-stinging white sands of White Sands National Monument. These millions are the inheritors of Yellowstone, whose sponsors never dreamed what they were setting in motion. Beginning with Yellowstone we took official cognizance that some parts of our world are unique, valuable, and irreplaceable. Part of our heritage. Part of the explanation for our being here and being the way we are. Part of our environment then and now. These are the parts that represent the richness and variety of life and history. Though Yellowstone caught us—and started us—with a wilderness mentality, fertility and so-called progress have forced us into looking at life and its surrounding natural wonders from the narrow vistas of sidewalks and windshields. By shifting our attitudes toward parks and places, by viewing Yellowstone as the origin point for a galvanic movement rather than a wonder fixed in time and geography, we can grow in sensitivity to our particular surroundings, whether the horizon is from here to infinity or from here to the next tenement alley.

Yellowstone started something. Ever since, men have tried to safeguard some of the best of what is, and what has been, even though it has meant giving quality priority over profit. Using Yellowstone as a starting block, we have been groping toward cooperating with our environment instead of forever and inflexibly demanding its unconditional surrender to our short-tempered and temporary needs and demands. We can exploit Yellowstone to make at least minimal movement toward pulling the veil from the eyes of our imprisoned city dweller to reveal to him that he, too, is a runner in the pursuit of happiness and that our national goals are his goals also.

In 1872 Yellowstone gave us a wide world of out-of-doors. In 1972 it points the way for crowded mankind to take his elbow from between his neighbor's ribs. Even if only for a moment, man needs to know that somewhere, some time, he can now and then breathe.

Western Impact on the Nation

Aʙᴏᴜᴛ a decade ago I was a speaker at a dinner sponsored by the University of Omaha for its Missouri Valley Conference on History. At that time I received an introduction which stands out, or burns, long after other introductions of more intrinsic worth have fused in my memory. My host, I think it was Stan Trickett, arose in his full dignity, which can be quite full, and told of the glories of Omaha—that it was from here that the wagon trains set out across the vast grasslands into the desert and mountains of the West; that it was from here that the first railroad to connect the East with the western seaboard began; that here was the upper terminus for most of the paddlewheel traffic on the Missouri River; that through here came the Mormons pushing their handcarts to Deseret; that across from here the Indians held their powwows on the Council Bluffs; and that even when transcontinental air traffic began in more

Delivered at the annual banquet of the Western History Association, Omaha, Nebraska, October 10, 1969, and published in the *Western Historical Quarterly* 1, no. 3 (July, 1970).

modern days, here was the first stop out of Chicago on the San Francisco and Los Angeles flights.

"Over the generations many people on their personal quests have passed through Omaha," he went on, "but at this dinner I give you a man who has spent a night in Omaha!"

His introduction is perhaps a ringing tribute to an otherwise pedestrian career. No identification, no building up, but practically an introduction equivalent to "Ladies and gentlemen, the President!" Or better still, "Ladies and gentlemen, Willie Mays!"

So I stand before you with less than usual humility, a distinguished American, distinguished not for his accomplishment in his chosen profession, but distinguished for having spent a night in Omaha. Those are my credentials, and in the next half hour or so you are going to see that I have used them with considerable presumption. Parenthetically, I should go back briefly and confess that the adjective for the phrase "chosen profession" was not selected with precision. I never chose history. I just sort of drifted into it with the usual lack of direction which characterizes my getting into anything.

In fact, while standing at this confessional, I should note that I did not choose to be here tonight. Evidently I was chosen by your Latter-Day Saints president, one Leonard J. Arrington, which means I have the sanction of the church, and as a result of a secular plot which renegade committeemen Phil Jordan, Bob Richmond, and Ben Procter foisted on Ted Grivas, your program chairman, who at that stage must have been desperate, indeed. What happened was that the program went for a latter-day professor, a recent president whose stock rises with each week of inaction in Washington. I am sure that shortly we will begin to see the latest variation of that quadrennial phenomenon, bumper stickers saying "I Even Miss Lyndon."

So what happened was that when the former president said no, it was too late to get an acceptable person as the Friday night speaker, and my reputation for willingness to sound off without preparation or substance being my one distinguishing feature, other than having spent a night in Omaha, my name was shoved before some hapless printer. The first time I knew my topic was when I received a printed program, which gives you some idea of the months of preparation which have gone into this bit of profundity which you are about to experience.

Except that it would rob me of a $5.75 per head captive audience, I could make one observation on western impact on the nation and close this thing down in a paragraph. Protocol and pride demand that I hang on a little longer, however.

These days I am spending most of my time in Washington, District of Columbia, the eastern auxiliary to the capital of the United States. The White House and the federal government have been captured by California and now lie somewhere outside Los Angeles. All of us have known that eventually Los Angeles would stretch to include all of the trans-Mississippi West, but we did not expect it to kidnap the nation's capital so quickly. In four weeks at San Clemente, or as a secretary of mine once spelled it in an error I have never been able to prove was not self-conscious, San Calamity, the president spent more weekends in the California White

House than he has in Washington since January 21. Since the government follows the president, San Clemente has won as handily and as overwhelmingly as if Ohio State had just taken the field against Slippery Rock. If that is not western impact, then I cannot deduce. The West has captured the nation. Eastern sophistication has been dulled, the South can no longer expect to rise again, nor for that matter will the sun rise again in the East. From now on the sun will rise in the West, and without predicting, it may set there also. The next roadshow movie will not be entitled "How the West Was Won," but "How the West Won"! All those surveyors, and all our founding fathers, and even Pierre L'Enfant wasted their time, or at best just did a temporary job in locating a capital. The remainder of the country will soon be minor league and satellite. Enough of whimsy.

Before me is an immense topic, in its way as immense as the region it is supposed to encompass. The West has been in man's consciousness ever since the first drunk turned outward instead of homeward at Jamestown. Tonight we concentrate our West beyond the Mississippi, or the ninety-eighth meridian, or just to the westward of San Clemente, depending on our particular breaking point. The impact of this area has produced schools of historians, has produced counter-schools of historians, and has produced neo-purists who have countered the counter-historians. They, too, are as endless as the prairies, but just as the prairies end in eventual mountains of grandeur, so we can hope that the re-re-revisionists will eventually blur into a mirage of grandeur. I doubt that they will produce grandeur with substance, but even the mirage would be as wel-

[48]

come as it is when it appears as the only evidence of wetness after crossing four hundred miles of West Texas desert land where you know the good Lord has just given up and is not going to try anymore.

What is the impact of the West upon the nation? Take your choice. If I wanted to be like some professors of history, I could start in detailing, and you would not get out of here until the next election. I could kill both history and this association with one long stroke. I will not be that pedantic, but let me mention a few details. The Whiskey Rebellion started in the then-West and helped to centralize our government. Evidencing the same dissatisfaction as their Pennsylvania counterparts, other farmers raised cane but no profitable wheat or corn on the flats of Kansas a century later. They were heard in Washington, and as we know, many a Populist demand was either accepted or revised and muted on a national basis.

In the West of the early national period, the Kentucky resolution spoke out for the freedom of man to speak out. More than a century later Big Bill Haywood spoke out with sentiments considered no more dangerous to the eastern establishment than those of the Kentuckians. Right now Berkeley is speaking to the nation, although no one is very clear as to what it is saying. Before Berkeley becomes serene, it will make its impact on considerably more than the educational scene in this nation.

The West of Jefferson's day gave us the grandiose, opaque scheme of Aaron Burr, the incomparable explorations of Lewis and Clark, and the comparable though still significant lesser explorations of men like

Zebulon Pike; and all of this, along with Napoleon's duplicity, gave us not only the real estate steal of the Louisiana Territory but an attitude toward loose construction of the Constitution by a strict constructionist, an attitude which has determined American outlook ever since. We have had, as you know, strict constructionists from Thomas Jefferson forward, but with Jefferson's leadership sparked by the enticements of the West, all strict constructionists have turned loose whenever desires and designs demanded it. As Justice Hugo Black has said on many occasions, "All problems start with the Constitution, and all decisions end with the Constitution." To which I might add, what happens in between is what determines the direction of this nation, and eventually the direction for you and for me. If Thomas Jefferson, who carried half the nation devotedly and emotionally in his wake, could have resisted the blandishments of the West and turned down Louisiana, he might have set a model for strict construction which could have prevailed. But he was human, and, being human, he was correct. In this respect the West then has had a continuing impact on the nation that has never let go.

So doggedly we proceed down the list of the presidents, each with his experience with the West—Madison and his War Hawks, Monroe with the problem of Missouri, Jackson with western banks and Indian removal, Polk with Texas and Oregon and the Mexican cession, Pierce buying an oversize section of western desert to help a railroad, Grant with his Indian policy and his transcontinental railroads and his founding of the first national park in the world at Yellowstone, Buchanan with silver, and Hayes with silver, and Benjamin Harrison with silver, and Cleveland with silver, and Cleveland and Harrison with demands of regulation of railroads and other large industries, and Harrison and Wilson with demands for women's rights, and that other Johnson and McKinley and Eisenhower with Alaska, and Theodore Roosevelt with the Japanese in California and with the conservation of western resources and always with railroads, and so on right up to the present.

Even a man whose administration was almost totally preoccupied with war and its concomitants, Abraham Lincoln, felt the western impact which eventuated in the Homestead Act and in granting western railroad concessions and financing. John Brown used the West as a dress rehearsal for Harper's Ferry, John J. Pershing used the Texas-Mexican border as a dress rehearsal for the American Expeditionary Force to Europe, and Nevada and New Mexico are currently being used as dress rehearsals for blowing up the world.

On the contrary side to the just-mentioned western War Hawks of Madison's day are the western isolationists of World War I and particularly of World War II. Without, for instance, William E. Borah's presence, Woodrow Wilson's task of unifying the western world and perhaps staving off World War II would have been easier. Without Senator Burton K. Wheeler's blindness to the fact that Montana was not the whole world, Franklin D. Roosevelt's task in preparing us for the Second World War would have been considerably facilitated. One of the continuing curiosities is that the South, almost invariably rigid on domestic issues, is liberal in its foreign attitudes, while the West is flexible on domestic issues but determinedly isolationist in foreign affairs.

That great turn-of-the-century adventure or aberration across the Pacific which gave us an empire in the Philippines and elsewhere was in part excused as being necessary to protect the West. Astoria on the Pacific helped create the nation's first great fortune for that erstwhile seller of tin flutes, John Jacob Astor. The nervous necessity for digging the Panama Canal was intensified by the need to shorten the commercial distance between Atlantic and Pacific harbors. In the process we raped an isthmus, but, unlike most rapes, that smirk on the face could almost be justified.

The West is contradictory. Almost two centuries after we thought we had disposed of theocracies and forever separated church and state—it said so in the Constitution—the Mormons came along to build a new combination church-state. Furthermore, they belong in the proper western genre. They not only built marvelously a society based on cooperation, but in the process bred some of the most vocally rampant individualists that this nation has produced, a cooperative society that believes vociferously in individualism.

Western humor has been worked over in thousands of books, articles, jokes, and scenarios. It is a humor based on exaggeration, mirroring exaggerated beneficences and deficiencies of the West. If the humor is not exaggerated, it is understated to the point of being as ridiculous as exaggeration. The West has been damned by an un-understanding East, which often mistakes the exaggeration for serious boasting. This gives the West an opportunity to feel aggrieved and misunderstood, and sometimes to feel unnecessarily sorry for itself. In turn, feeling sorry for yourself can lead to demands which have to be heard, and western demands are heard in disproportion to population. The crybaby always gets the pacifier.

The penchant for violence in the West is well known, or can't you find a TV repairman? From the beginning the frontier has been associated with violence and with law-breaking. We have always admired the man who took direct action. "Let's try the S.O.B., and then let's hang him!" The South has been rightly damned for lynch law, but the West could show it a few tricks. In fact, the West didn't even have racial arrogance as justification. But the West concealed its lynch laws and its Ku Klux Klan by calling it and them vigilantism and vigilantes. But as in the South, such extracurricular violence was justified as necessary for law and order and keeping rascals of whatever hue in their places. And in the process we make heroes out of the violators.

Listen to this:

On September 26, 1872, three mounted men rode up to the gate of the Kansas City fair, which was enjoying a huge crowd of perhaps 10,000 people. Bandits shot at the ticket seller, hit a small girl in the leg, and made off for the woods with something less than a thousand dollars. It was highhanded, and it endangered the lives of a whole host of holiday minded people for comparatively little reward.

What makes the robbery and the violence notable is not the crime itself but the way it was reported in the Kansas City *Times* by one John N. Edwards. In his front-page story, he branded the robbery "so diabolically daring and so utterly in contempt of fear that we are bound to admire and revere its perpetrators."

Two days later the outlaws were being compared by the *Times* with the Knights of King Arthur's Round Table: "It was as though three bandits had come to us from storied Odenwald, with the halo of medieval chivalry upon their garments and shown us how the things were done that poets sing of. Nowhere else in the United States or in the civilized world, probably, could this thing have been done."[1]

Only in America! Only in the West!

About the same time that this epic event was being perpetrated, census statistics for 1880 revealed that Leadville, Colorado, with a population of 14,820, had one hundred houses of prostitution, or one house for every 148 persons—man, woman, and child. Eliminating women and children, which would take more work than I care to go into, that means one house for every fifty adult males. That is what I call western service!

Contrast that with the figures for Boston, which had one hundred houses for a population of 362,839. That boils down to one house for every 725 probable adult males. Perhaps that is why the westerner considers Boston to be effete (to employ a word that most westerners would never use).

Of course, a considerable case could be made for the probity of San Francisco at this time. With a population of 233,959, its statistics show no houses—I repeat, zero houses of prostitution. This suggests, as the author I'm plagiarizing wryly points out, that in some cities

[1] Quoted from Joe B. Frantz, "The Frontier Tradition: An Invitation to Violence," in *The History of Violence in America: Historical and Comparative Perspectives*, ed. Hugh Davis Graham and Ted Robert Gurr (New York, 1968), pp. 127–128.

crime statistics in 1880 were no more accurate than they are in 1969.[2]

But it is no secret, not what God can do, but how the West winked at violence, as long as it was carried out within certain ground rules. Billy the Kid was a pathological, paranoid punk, but because he shot men down he is canonized. Pat Garrett finally dispatched him from this free world by ambushing him in the dark, which leaves us not quite sure about the beatification of Pat. If he had gunned Billy down in a fight in which Billy had a chance to fire back, Pat would rank high alongside other possible murderers like Hickok and Earp. (Of course, with my sensitive stomach I have always excused Earp. Any man with a name like that ought to harbor resentments and strike out blindly now and then!)

Undeniably the code of the West condoned violence. Adultery might be sufficient reason for hanging a man, even though the adulterer would have been happy to have continued life, and the adultered might even have been willing to be sinned against again. (In this case, I guess you really *are* sinned against.) But shooting under the proper rules is permissible. Burning down a sheepherder's hut was permissible. Chivington massacring Indian women and children raised a dubious hero. Custer vowing to take no prisoners has become even more holy. So long as somebody died perforated, the deed could be excused. This is an impact of the West which concerns us nationally more in 1969 than it did in 1869. How do you preserve man's freedom to defend

2 Frank Richard Prassel, *The Western Peace Officer: A Legacy of Law and Order* (Norman: University of Oklahoma Press, 1972), pp. 7–8.

himself, his right as an individual to bear arms, and not turn loose every quick-tempered hotspur to maim and to kill?

Not that violence is an exclusive property of the West. Not that it ever was. Recently in Maryland, just over the line from the District of Columbia, a local mass meeting was held to discuss the registration of guns. In came the solid citizens—white shirts, ties, and $150 suits. Hair was cut short, faces were eligible for and smelled of shaving lotion, and no one had to sit apart for lack of bathing. And then the problem was opened for discussion.

No student militant storming the gate outside Fayerweather Hall at Columbia or Black Panther slithering down the alleys of Oakland ever showed more hate, more extremism, less disposition to listen, less tolerance for opposing viewpoints or even for pleas of moderation. A near riot ensued. Everyone tried to shout down everyone else. They seethed and they shouted and they threatened. They would kill each other for their right to have guns for peace. And then, I suppose, they all went home, watched Lawrence Welk, and asked what the young people are coming to! No, the West does not alone hold violence in its hand, but the West has glamorized it, and men of the West have made it palatable among so-called decent folk. Palatable—but likely to choke.

From all history textbooks you know the impact of the post–Civil War West on the country—the final laying of the Indian threat, the building of the transcontinental railroads, the conquering of the great American desert, the further rise of mining interests, the growth of the cattle kingdom, and so on. These factors in completing the settlement of the nation are too elementary to be recounted here, though certain facets might be mentioned. The Indian threat gave us a standing army in the West, which pumped federal money into the area and assured a moving economy. The presence of the army and the Indians also gave us excuses to shoot, either as soldiers or as private citizens, with the true Americanism of violence.

The coming of the railroads to the West, the sophistication of mining techniques, and the creation of giant cattle spreads held out lures of great profits, lures which stretched across the Atlantic. The result was an infusion of foreign money—principally Scottish, English, and Dutch—into the United States, so that all that eastern money was free for other types of development and exploitation. Echoing Bernard Shaw's father in *Misalliance,* "Read Clark Spence; read Turpy Jackson!" The West then proved an effective seducer of outside capital, as well as an equally effective seducer of immigrant peoples. The West attracted central and northern Europeans as never before, with the possible exception of those Germans who fled the dissatisfactions about 1848, and likewise the West attracted immigrants from the Orient. Already occupying the West were men of Spanish or Indian extraction, or both, so that the West soon presented its own form of cosmopolitanism, a delightful discovery to all those people in the East who look on the West as a gathering of homogeneous, insular patches.

Everyone knows the road to exclusion of Orientals in those unenlightened days around the close of the past century and the beginning of this one. The West Coast states took the leadership. But in a more recent era, the California delegation on January 22, 1934, wrote Franklin D. Roosevelt opposing any dilution of the Japanese Exclusion Act of ten years earlier. Its reason is at least candid and not masked behind presumably humane, economic reasons. What the delegation charged was that Japan really "insists on a status of 'equality' as to immigration with white countries." Less than three weeks later the Washington-Oregon delegation wrote the president that it too "vigorously opposed" abolition of the exclusion policy. One of the signers was a name later nationally prominent, the honorable Mon C. Wallgren of the second district, State of Washington. Roosevelt sent a note asking "the most responsible of the California congressmen to come and see" him. But when Undersecretary of State William Phillips noted that "it was no part of the intention of the Administration to bring this question up," the question was dropped. What later happened to the West Coast Japanese in World War II is a blot whose presence will always remind us that concentration camps are not confined to Nazis.

To look at another facet, the West is not unlike the South in returning people to national office, so that key chairmanships in both houses of Congress are frequently held by westerners, often with as stultifying results as occur from southern leadership. For example, speaking of key chairmanships, Senator Key Pittman of Nevada was Franklin Roosevelt's chairman of the Senate Foreign Relations Committee. In time Senator Pittman moved on, and Roosevelt worked with Tom Connally of Texas. J. William Fulbright, from a trans-Mississippi state, though personally more identified with the South than the West, was placed on the Foreign Relations Committee by a western Senate majority leader named Lyndon Johnson, who in time inherited Senator Fulbright as *his* chairman on the Foreign Relations Committee. Perhaps Fulbright's attitudes reflect a key—that word again—western attitude, despite his southernness: principle should prevail over gratitude. I am sure that former President Johnson would see little gratitude in Fulbright's conduct of hearings!

We have mentioned Burton K. Wheeler; in 1933 he teamed up with Senator Elmer Thomas of Oklahoma to try to persuade President Franklin Roosevelt to send that most noisome and noxious of radio priests, Father Charles E. Coughlin of Detroit, as economic adviser to the American delegation at the economic conference in London later that summer. Some economist! The pressure, thank the Lord, was insufficient to overcome FDR's good judgment. In a period of liberating the country from the high-tariff policy of previous Republican administrations, President Roosevelt again was bedeviled by Governor Tom Berry of South Dakota, not for retention of a high tariff, but for a flat embargo on blackstrap molasses. On the other hand, Nebraska's Senator George Norris, a long way from any water except the erratic Platte and Missouri, led the Senate fight for ratification of the Saint Lawrence Waterways Treaty in 1934 and is generally acknowledged as the spiritual father of the Tennessee Valley Authority, a good thousand miles from the state he represented. It was no accident that a New Yorker named Theodore Roosevelt made conservation of natural resources respectable. After all, he was sentimentally a North Dakota rancher who understood what leadership from the East had long overlooked.

In later days, men like Senator Henry Jackson, chairman of the Committee on Interior and Insular Affairs; Carl Hayden, until recently chairman of the Senate Appropriations Committee; the late Senator Clare Engle of California; Senator Clinton Anderson of New Mexico; former Senator Thomas H. Kuchel of California; and Congressman Wayne Aspinall of Colorado have presented the problems of the West to a national audience in a way that could be understood.

Most of our secretaries of the interior and of agriculture have had at least a western background. Under Lyndon B. Johnson of Texas, Stewart Udall of Arizona served the second longest tenure as secretary of the interior for the Democrats; when they left office in 1969, President Richard Nixon of California named an even farther westerner, former Governor Walter Hickel from Alaska. Notably, both secretaries have agreed on one policy. Interior is no longer primarily a conserver of western resources, picturesque and economic. Our national parks, monuments, historic landmarks, recreation areas, and so on, should go to the people. If they can't go to the people, then bring the people to them. Both secretaries, both westerners under western presidents, have turned eastward in their thinking. This attitude is bipartisan, nonregional, and abundantly necessary.

When, for example, in his conservation message of February, 1965, President Johnson proposed using land and water conservation funds to acquire land for twelve additions of national stature, five of the twelve lay east of the Mississippi—Assateague Island National Seashore,

Tocks Island National Recreation Area, Cape Lookout National Seashore, Sleeping Bear Dunes National Lakeshore, and Indiana Dunes National Lakeshore. The near monopoly on scenic wonders which the West once held just no longer pertains.

Oh sure, the West still holds its enormous variety of natural resources. Copper, petroleum, potentially valuable oil shale, nowadays hydroelectric power, and timber all make the West precious. Quite naturally, one of our largest national scandals centered on the petroleum at Teapot Dome. Again, it is notable that when tariffs were being generally reduced, the tariff on wool usually remained intact. The livestock industry accounts for one-third of this nation's agricultural income, and the West has a livestock tradition. The West has made its power felt in the 27½ percent oil depletion allowance. Despite the fact that this allowance is going to be reduced in the administration of a president from California, the thrust for reduction comes less from the trans-Mississippi states than from the cis-Mississippi area.

Since many of the problems once considered basically western have now become national, the West can no longer claim exclusive interest. We have mentioned labor radicalism. The first big black riot of current time occurred in the Watts section of Los Angeles, but it broke beyond Los Angeles to hit cities throughout the nation. In fact, at the height of the Watts disturbance President Johnson was observing to guests on the opposite coast, "those of you in the District of Columbia, I want to warn you this morning that the clock is ticking, time is moving, that we should and we must ask ourselves every night when we go home: Are we doing all we should do in our Nation's Capital, and all the other big cities of the country where 88 percent of the population of this country is going to be living in the year 2000?"[3]

And in a news conference that same day President Johnson observed that "in Los Angeles we found that we could not contain disappointment and the frustrations," and indicated to the discomfiture of some people that the problems of Los Angeles were simply symptoms of a disease that would appear on a national scale.[4] It did.

On a happier note, once the West was land where the air was fresh and clean. In this Year of our Lord 1969, three-fourths of the eight million people in the Los Angeles area are annoyed by severe eye irritation much of the year. In this case the West has joined the East in a grand design for pollution. The wind still blows, but it had darn' sure better be from the right direction. Not all of the fog that hangs over Tony Bennett's San Francisco comes rolling in from the Pacific. Denver, sitting a dry mile high, sometimes has its own industrial cloud as thick as Saint Louis, Pittsburgh, or Charlotte has. Jets fly high over delicate, isolated Arizona canyons, and the ripping roar tears thin slabs from sheer rock walls carved painstakingly by nature and sometimes decorated by Indians. This is free air? No, air and water pollution are not confined to the crowded industrial East. Eyes are as likely to smart in Moab as

3 *Public Papers of the Presidents of the United States: Lyndon B. Johnson, 1965* (Washington: Government Printing Office, 1966), p. 932.
4 Ibid., p. 936.

they are in Maine, but the minds seem to be no smarter. The West now has the same propensity for cluttering as does the East. West Yellowstone, Montana, and Virginia City, Nevada, are as tinseled and spurious as Gatlinburg and Coney Island.

To quote President Johnson again, "We have placed a wall of civilization between us and between the beauty of our land and of our countryside. In our eagerness to expand and to improve, we have relegated nature to a weekend role, and we have banished it from our daily lives."[5]

Yet that is not entirely true or fair. We still have our vast portions of untouched scenery, looking much as it did when Lewis and Clark first nosed against its banks. And we have intelligent people trying to utilize our wonders. Thus, Arizona has arranged miles of irrigation and canal banks to be used by riders and hikers. In New Mexico utility rights-of-way are used for public trails. In Montana the Missouri runs for one hundred miles in country free, virgin, and almost wild. And yet the West still has its stark grandeur, complete and replete with urban problems. During its summer season, Yellowstone has bumper-to-bumper traffic, and its high mountain air smells more of carburetor fumes than pine smoke; Yosemite is as much a hippie haven as Haight-Ashbury, Lincoln Park in Chicago, or Georgetown in Washington. Meanwhile, still quoting, "people move out from the city to get closer to nature only to find that nature has moved farther from them."[6]

Along that line, once you could tell a westerner by

5 Ibid., p. 1073.
6 Ibid., p. 155.

his leathery tanned face and the squint wrinkles around his eyes. Nowadays he wears large dark glasses which eliminate the squint, rides in air-conditioned station wagons, leaves his house only to go to the barbecue pit, and is more likely to be pale than his Connecticut neighbor, who seizes every moment of weak sun on 60-degree days to don his sweater and bathing trunks and freeze at the beach.

The West has shown the way in international agreements, perhaps because it has had international problems. Thus, under the leadership of Presidents Kennedy and Johnson, Texas and northern Mexico successfully settled the Chamizal problem after a century of cat-fighting. Thus, the agreement was reached with Mexico in March, 1965, relating to the Colorado River salinity problem. Thus the International Boundary and Water Commission for the United States and Mexico. Thus the recent dedication of the Amistad Dam and National Recreation Area on the Rio Grande. Thus the Columbia River Treaty between the United States and Canada under which that great river will be cooperatively developed. Despite its tradition of one-man, simple rifle justice, the West has never developed unilaterally. Its problems always involved others, and others had to agree, whether they were Indians trying to remain free, miners and ranchers disputing over water rights, or Mexican nationals trying to hold on to a receding land.

Again, the West once believed that it alone yearned for water. It scanned the clear skies and prayed to isolated bits of cumulus as fervently as an Arab. Students on both sides of the Mississippi knew that a millennium ago in the Arizona country the Indians had built extensive waterworks, not unlike those we build now. They irrigated the land, and they made the desert flower as surely as the Mormons transformed their basin. But dams are no good when it does not rain, and droughts were prolonged, and the Indians seemed to have dried up with the land. This is an interesting story to hear from a National Park Service interpreter at Mesa Verde, but from a practical standpoint it is of concern only to the diminishing farmer and rancher. To the metropolitan politician it could not have mattered less.

When toward the close of that seven-year drought in the Southwest in the 1950's President Dwight Eisenhower flew to the area and exhibited a concern born of a boyhood in Kansas, eastern pundits treated Eisenhower's sympathy for the conditions as an isolated phenomenon. So, a few cows were going to get dehydrated![7]

But with the increasing complexity of our urban society, not to mention what Wallace Stegner calls our "incontinent fertility," water today is a nationwide problem and not an exclusive western one. From the Potomac to the Penobscot the East had its drought in the 1960's. Water tables dropped, water rationing took place, and a land of plenty and gentility began to hear what the raw, arid West had been talking to the wind about. Finally, interstate conferences were called, as governors of New Jersey talked with governors of Massachusetts about the scarcity of water. Water, the

7 Ibid., p. 866.

concern solely of the West, had now transported its problems across the nation. Even the alligators died off in the Everglades for want of water.

Therefore, all the nation knew what President Johnson was talking about when in dedicating the Sam Rayburn Dam in Texas in May, 1965, he intoned the following:

> No single resource is more important to us than water. Our management of the American water resources is basic to the success in meeting the many obligations and opportunities of our growing population.
>
> Water has always been the first concern of the West and Southwest States. Today, no region in the Nation can afford to take water for granted because from the Atlantic to the Pacific coast the urbanization and the industrialization are creating a mighty and great thirst for water and more water. . . . If this thirst is not satisfied by positive and constructive and timely action, we could experience very grave trouble in fulfilling the promises and potentials of American life.[8]

And again all sections nodded approvingly when later in the year, while signing the authorization of the Auburn-Folsom Project in California, the president remarked, "I have never seen a dollar invested anywhere in this nation in water conservation, in multiple-use projects, that in the period of even a decade didn't prove that it was a good investment, and would pay very high returns on what we had spent for it."

So if water and climate and clean air and resources and interior projects no longer represent the impact of the West, and if there is as much variance in, say,

8 Ibid., p. 510.

western secretaries of agriculture as there was between Henry Wallace of Iowa and Ezra Taft Benson from Utah, then what *is* the enduring, exclusive impact of the West on the nation?

To my mind the impact goes back to a place of space and natural resources. The West had, and has, space despite its being the most urbanized region of our nation. Space reacts on mankind like pool halls did on River City's musical salesman—it spells something, only in this case it is Opportunity instead of Trouble. With all that space, something just has to happen periodically. The West holds a self-renewing lottery ticket. When one payoff plays out, a new ticket will pop up elsewhere, and it is back to the mutuel window.

Right now Alaska has won the latest lottery, the whole works, the Daily Double. The Quinella. The Sweepstakes. Soon ships will crush the ice barriers of the Northwest Passage. Pipelines will be laid for thousands of miles, and heated oil will melt the permafrost of the tundra as it courses through from the frozen world to the consuming world. In the process they will probably chase off the caribou and rearrange the ecology of a whole subcontinent. Eskimos will get rich, if for no better reason than for serving the tavern needs of roughnecks from the oil fields of Florida and Louisiana. They will all eat convenience foods and will leave greasy wrappers and soft drink cans for the anthropologists. Some Eskimo girl will emerge as the Princess of Point Barrow simply by sharing in traditionally western neighborly fashion the endowment which God gave her.

Every time the nation feels that it has closed all its economic frontiers, that the only way to advance is through the slow, careful accretion of capital and principal, based on the time-honored standards of some State Street trust conservator in Boston, the West throws in a rich lagniappe so unexpected as to be almost totally intoxicating. No wonder that the West has disdained government planning for enlarged gross national product. It is as childishly believing as a broke horse player. After all, when it finally does rain in the West, it comes a gully-washer, a cloudburst. When oil is found, it gushes. When silver is mined, it is the Comstock.

As with weather, so with economics. The Dust Bowl victims of the 1930's, with their hollow-eyed children, gaunt women, and rickety old trucks, now sit in a country club in Amarillo or Oklahoma City and feel no historic kinship with the hungry Navajo still trying to grub it out. We sweated it, they claim, and you can sweat it, too. Generations of poverty and generations of denial need not be corrected; if you have not progressed, it must be through lack of faith. Or so they seem to say.

Then to a great extent the western impact is philosophical. The philosophy that commingles despair with blind optimism. Call it a belief in progress, if you prefer. We have long worshiped at the altar of progress, and thereby justified many an excess. But because the West was out there to give us unanticipated riches, we have believed in progress, perhaps undeserved riches, certainly unregulated riches. Just a quarter-century ago, here came uranium, not to mention the windfalls of federally supported airspace and electronics developments. Now it's petroleum in Alaska, and the stock exchange in Anchorage will become as frenzied as San Francisco's or New York's. Shortly there will be a Petroleum Club in Fairbanks, and a new breed of wealthy will sit around and discuss over Chivas Regal and soda how quickly and surely this nation is going to the dogs.

This does not matter. What matters is that once again the West has come through to reinforce the American dream. We cannot all go to Alaska, and most of the people who go will not get rich. But at a time of national discontent with overwhelming social problems, we can, some of us, delay hard solution. We do not have to listen to the reformers, to the alarmists, not even to the moderates. Our hero is Mr. Micawber. Something has turned up. Sweat awhile, worry awhile, and something else will turn up. When we cannot tolerate some situation any longer, the West, like the Lord, will provide.

This then, is the impact of the West. A beacon to the world illuminating the belief that progress is accidental and miraculous and unplanned. Sure, there are extras like unbridled individualism. But the West's message to the world and to the nation is the message of the old prospector always looking for one more stake, always dreaming of rich veins that never run out, always more interested in moving with hope than with intelligence.

The West has given the nation a faith in unplanned progress. Despite the heady pleasure of an occasional bonanza, this impact is not an unmixed blessing.

The American West:
Child of Federal Subsidy

WHEN I accepted this assignment and arbitrarily picked a title, like everyone else I did not suspect the events of that long, lost weekend in November when we all died a little from the assassin's bullet; when we sat horrified by televised vigilante justice, western-style; when those of us who are historians and teachers watched our ideals and illusions and youth drain away with a President's blood as we asked ourselves, "Is this all we have taught? Is this all we have learned?" Suddenly we were unbearably old and desiccated and weary.

As the ebb tide of hope reversed and we began to pick up again, the temptation to take a new topic, as far away as possible from a West that includes my native Texas, became almost overpowering. And yet at the same time the desire of people everywhere to judge, to place guilt, to indulge in emotional, sometimes

Delivered before the annual meeting of the American Historical Association, December 28, 1963, and published in part in *The Progressive* 28 (Oct., 1964) and the *Texas Observer* 64 (May 1, 1964) and in whole in the *Congressional Record*, March 18, 1964.

maudlin self-incrimination that does little service to the memory of John F. Kennedy makes me drop my western defensiveness while refusing to go on the attack.

No longer must I endure being introduced in out-of-state meetings to the accompaniment of some pleasantly extravagant Texas jokes. Such jokes are no longer even acidly funny. For a synthetic Texas tradition ended that day, and now Texans may become people, like everyone else, with some good and some bad, some smart and some stupid, some reticent and some loud-mouthed, and some national and rational and some parochial and emotional. And some enlightened day we may even be able to life the national restriction on playing the song "Are You from Big D?" and enjoy being most happy fellas with a town which probably has as high a percentage of decent sorts as anywhere else.

So the title picked in the summer of 1963 fits after all, even though that is a distant age when we were innocent and convinced of our self-importance. And in the title a question inheres: Is the tradition of a West where men stood alone against their environment, asking no help from anyone, and least of all their government—is that tradition tenable? When that long-legged son-of-a-gun stands up in a cattleman's club in Cheyenne, or in a chamber of commerce banquet in Tucson, or at a governors' conference in Helena, and when he issues a blast at an all-consuming federal encroachment in words more blistering than all the winds that blow from Spokane to San Antonio, is he historically sound, or has he swallowed a whole hunk of home-manufactured, self-illuminated halo without chewing it first?

[71]

Not for a moment do I deny my fellow westerner his due. He triumphed—and triumphs—over environmental obstacles that develop a man, that make him self-reliant, that give him understanding and patience, and that let him know that individual and collective success is possible.

But he is—West or East—first of all a man and therefore acquisitive, and angling, and insecure, and as full of resolves as some of us on each January 1. Every time he thinks he knows all the answers, as many of us did before noon last November 22, something cataclysmic comes along to remind him that he sits tall in the saddle only when he has a saddle to sit in and a horse to put it on. The cataclysm may be truly that—the San Francisco earthquake and fire—or it may be as small as grasshoppers or as big as a sky that blazes day in and day out without a cloud to seed, or it may be a bank in straits having to call his note. But whatever it is, whenever those personal catastrophes hit, the westerner acts, and has acted, just like a human being and will take help wherever he can get it.

And yet two years later when the wheat is waving and the cattle are fat and the silver veins are all high-grade, or closing Suez has caused an oil shortage in Europe, our western friend will deny by all the saints (if he can think of two, he's in good shape)—he will deny that anyone manufactured this prosperity except himself and the good Lord, who overendowed him with cunning and astuteness and Christian virtues and, most of all, a knowledge that there is no substitute for hard work. (Gad, until I mentioned hard work I thought I was describing myself.) Or as Jim Ferguson used to admonish voters, "You have only three friends in the world—God Almighty, Sears Roebuck, and Jim Ferguson."

But let's get on with the academic paraphernalia and document a little. According to the Texas Education Agency's economic index for 1963–1964, the state's value added by manufactures totaled $5.5 billion; the value of its minerals was $4.2 billion; of its agriculture, $2.25 billion; and its payrolls, $4.75 billion. The state's assessed valuation exceeded $12.5 billion. Incomplete data for 1962 indicate that the federal government spent $3.75 billion in Texas, including $0.5 billion in federal aid (Texas, as you can see, like all western states looks on all federal aid as spiritually corrosive and so holds the bill down), $1.33 billion in federal salaries, and better than $1 billion in prime military contracts.

Is Texas subsidized? We wouldn't think of it for a moment.

But why pick on Texas, or suffer the implications of mid-century welfarism? Let's retreat, as so many of us would like to do, to the rugged individualist days of nearly a century ago: "There is nothing so little thought of in this part of the country as a soldier," Paul Sharp quotes a latter-nineteenth-century Montanan as saying. "There are only two creatures who look upon a soldier here without scorn and contempt, and they are little children and dogs."[1] And yet it was the presence of these

[1] Paul F. Sharp, *Whoop-Up Country: The Canadian-American West, 1865–1885* (Minneapolis: University of Minnesota Press, 1955), p. 127.

contemptible soldiers which not only brought services to such isolated areas as Forts Benton and Shaw, but markets as well. As Sharp points out:

> The construction of these northern posts speeded the economic development of the region. Government spending to construct and maintain the forts introduced considerable currency into this frontier region. Army quartermaster purchases of fresh vegetables, butter, eggs, hay, and grain stimulated the initial agricultural enterprise in the Sun River Valley and in the rich alluvial bottom lands along the Missouri River. Heavy purchases of beef to feed thousands of soldiers prompted the rapid expansion of the range cattle industry on the benchlands and surrounding plains.
>
> Army troops, recruited in the East and transferred to the West at Government expense, provided a labor force for the region. This manpower built roads, telegraph lines, bridges, and other public works and established extensive farms around the posts.
>
> Army expenditures played such an important role in the region's economy that citizens constantly implored the Government to expand its military commitments. They often pictured friendly Indians as hostile and exaggerated isolated depredations into a state of warfare.[2]

And Sharp adds that government spending even provided Montana with opportunities for fraud. What greater service could a government render an individualist?

In fact, around Fort Benton, not only the federal government in Washington but the Canadian government in Ottawa extended its strangling influence. Ac-

2 Ibid., p. 128.

cording to Sharp, when the Northwest Mounted Police got their man just beyond the border, they "created a heavy demand for provisions and supplies, for cash funds and credit facilities,"[3] which could not be met out of Canada. Treaties with Indians merely heightened the demand for goods and services, so that the decade of the 1870's, which had begun in a special Montana misery, ended on a glorious economic plateau that convinced each Montana merchant that he had done it all himself.

Meanwhile, in Washington Major Martin Maginnis, representing the Montanans, successfully fought any threat of reduction of expenditures to Indians or consolidation of Indian agencies because such efficient action would hurt Montana trade. (Any similarity between Maginnis' views and those of outraged congressmen these past few months over Secretary McNamara's closing of certain military installations just goes to show how much we learn from articles like this.)

And in 1963 in Texas the *Dallas Morning News,* which had fought bravely against wasting public moneys on such useless socialistic boondoggles as the Saint Lawrence Seaway, and which until the spring of 1963 thought that the only thing more prodigal than Senator Ralph Yarborough was Lyndon B. Johnson, suddenly hails the then vice-president and the New Frontier for its courage and vision in approaching the silvery, serpentine, waterless Trinity River canal project, which proposes to make Dallas a seaport despite its position 294 miles from the nearest ocean wave. But subsidy, never.

[3] Ibid., p. 212.

To stay contemporaneous for another moment, about 1957 Gene Hollon queried eight United States senators from the Oklahoma, Texas, New Mexico, and Arizona area about the reasons for political pressures they received from their constituents.[4] Without exception they listed reclamation aid, public power through rural electrification, flood control, and various aspects of the water problem. Hollon's figures show that of the eighty-three federally built reservoirs in 1957, one-fourth (how do you get one-fourth of eighty-three?) — one-fourth of them were located in those same four states, despite their having only one-tenth of the population of the nation.

And the *Arizona Business and Economic Review,* hardly dedicated to the welfare state, opines as how a relatively large percentage of Arizona's income and employment is a result of government work and suggests that greater industrial diversification is the answer to bringing Arizona's dependence on federal subsidy down to the happy proximity of the national average.

But in a later article the same publication shows how Arizona's industrial development has leaned in the latter days on the Parker and Hoover dams, and how three projected dams—Bridge Canyon, Marble Canyon, and Glen Canyon—hold the key to continued economic enhancement. The *Review* calls for more power projects, while at the same time it observes historically that after passage of the Boulder Canyon Project Act of 1928 Arizona's attitude of hostility to-

4 W. Eugene Hollon, *The Southwest: Old and New* (New York: Alfred A. Knopf, 1961), pp. 362–363.

ward the Colorado River power projects was ignorant and reckless.

And meanwhile, one of Arizona's favorite sons can say with a perfectly straight political face that he favors federal subsidization of Arizona reclamation and power projects while announcing that in the Great American East such projects are rank un-American socialism. In other words, what is socialism in Tennessee is called necessity in Arizona.

Next door in New Mexico we find essentially the same situation: arid land, low population ratio, and dependence on mining and ranching—one extracting and self-defeating and the other dedicated to boom-or-bust procedures. But in the view of one business critic, the burdens of the future are already being lightened by the presence of a new, envigorating business—the military. Even though a certain amount of administrative and congressional whim is involved in such hypodermics as Los Alamos, our critic believes that such risk is acceptable, and goes on to say that the value of reclamation and flood control improvements resulting from military influence is nearly equal to improved soil and water conservation.

The truth is that the federal government is the major stockholder and underwriter of the American West and that most of those portions of the West which hum with economic excitement are constantly being replenished with federal funds. The California story is a larger, richer edition of the Texas experience. As of June 30, 1955, the federal government owned 87 percent of the land in Nevada—almost nine out of every ten acres—70 percent in Utah; 65 percent in Idaho; and 51 percent in Oregon. And in the eighteen years prior to 1955 the government's purchase of lands was running 255 percent ahead of its sales. The percentage of federal ownership in the West, in other words, is climbing. No wonder, then, that many politicians and private entrepreneurs view the federal government as ubiquitous. But to deny that ubiquity does not promote subsidy, and to argue that the West is the one region where man still stands alone is sheer refusal to face facts.

In all fairness it should be said that not all Westerners make such a mistake. In the *Oregon Business Review* in late 1957, for example, the statement is made that "since 1910, growth of population and income in the Pacific Northwest has been at or below the national rate of growth except . . . when . . . stimulated by heavy Federal expenditures" on such developments as aircraft installations, missile production, expansion in lumber and pulp production, aluminum fabrication, and hydroelectric power.[5] The Hanford Atomic Works in eastern Washington, once a blighted and isolated area, represents three-quarters of Washington's employment in chemical activities, not to mention up to fifteen thousand construction workers that have been used since World War II. Federal help with fisheries, with highways, and with irrigation could also be included.

The list of historic federal subsidies to the West is inclusive, widespread, and, in its broad outlines, well

5 James N. Tattersall, "River Basin Development Vital for Economic Growth of Northwest," *Oregon Business Review* 16 (Oct., 1957): 1–4.

known. Land grants to railroads, cattlemen grazing on almost limitless public domain, mineral rights claimed by whoever got there first and could make his claim stick, the Gadsden Purchase to facilitate a railroad route, guarantees of silver purchase, subsidized stagecoach routes, exploratory expeditions from Lewis and Clark forward, forts by the dozen (of 169 posts in the United States, 130 were in the West), wagon roads, dredged harbors, Indian relief, agricultural experimentation, homesteads, Timber Culture Act, Desert Land Act, frontier donations, land-grant colleges, a Panama Canal to bring western goods closer to the consuming centers, support of tourism through federally supported parks and monuments—the list isn't interminable, but it is long. Let's refresh ourselves on a few items, some without comment:

Brigham Young, leader of those almost fiercely independent, cooperative, antigovernment sons of Moroni, apparently thought about a Pacific railroad as early as 1847–1848. By 1852 the Mormon territorial legislature in Utah was memorializing Congress to construct a railroad to the Pacific. Later the church leaders themselves sent a similar petition.

In a day when market research and other aids to 'way out yonder were unheard of, much less perfected, the federal government sponsored the four so-called Great Surveys of the West between 1867 and 1879, two by the War Department and two by the Department of the Interior. They were great, says their biographer, not only "in the sense of the vast territories they examined," but also because they "built up the knowledge which establishes the habits of millions of Americans, shapes their businesses, and in fact makes possible the way they live."[6] And though the knowledge was broadcast, the individuals picking up the seeds here and there thought somehow that they had conceived each seed themselves.

And Russell, Majors, and Waddell spread their enterprise across the Great West, American entrepreneurs in both a classic and romantic tradition. But historians of the West are becoming more and more aware that the freighting empire those three built would have been nothing without the assistance of federal money.

Long before Alexander Majors struck out (to employ a verb you can translate two ways), the United States Army had been designated as roadbuilder for the West. All western roads became military roads—they were deemed necessary for the defense of the West against its enemies. (Generally speaking, they still are.) Along with the building of wagon roads, the army engineers gathered considerable topographical information which would prove invaluable when rugged individualists like Jay Gould and Collis P. Huntington, subsidized in part by federal funds, would lay their ties across the West.

"The achievements of the Topographical Engineers were considerable," writes one author:

In the realm of practical service they explored the important trails, located passes through the mountains, and supervised the construction of roads (both local and transcontinental). They totaled up the national resources.

[6] Richard A. Bartlett, *Great Surveys of the American West* (Norman: University of Oklahoma Press, 1962), pp. xiv–xv.

They prospected for water and minerals. They surveyed the possibilities of agriculture, and they helped to brush aside the Indian barrier. They mapped most of the major rivers and on several occasions supervised their improvement projects. They surveyed the important harbors, built dams, constructed lighthouses, and laid out coastal fortifications. In all of these operations they invested their skills and the extensive federal subsidies in an undeveloped region at a time when the settlers themselves were unable to do so.[7]

Now I can belabor my point, detailing demands by Kansas farmers for federal relief from drought and grasshoppers, outlining the guarantees under the Sherman Silver Purchase Act, reciting what the 27½ percent depletion allowance has meant to Western oil exploration, and even putting in a good word for Texas A&M by showing how that federal land-grant college eradicated the Texas tick, thereby adding millions to the income of Texas cattlemen.

But if the point hasn't been made by now, it won't be. The Westerner can rear up on his hindlegs—r'ar up on his hin' laigs, to be more nearly precise—and shout that he and he alone wrested that land from the desert or wind or Indian or whatever possessed it. But the truth is that from start to finish he was subsidized from his brogans to his sombrero and that further research may well prove that of the three or four historic regions in this sectionalized land of ours, his was the one which received—and still receives—the most assistance from a federal government which was sometimes benign, some-

[7] William H. Goetzmann, *Army Exploration in the American West, 1803–1863* (New Haven: Yale University Press, 1959), p. 430.

times misdirected, sometimes wasteful, and sometimes dictatorial, but which always, like a watching parent, was there.

Truth then compels us from the West to admit our debt, and to recognize that the poet, Badger Clark, replete with western sentiment though he was, spoke wisdom when he wrote:

> 'Twas good to live when all the sod,
> Without no fence nor fuss,
> Belonged in pardnership to God,
> The Gover'ment and us.[8]

[8] Charles Badger Clark, "The Old Cow Man," *Sun and Saddle Leather*, 5th ed. (Boston: Richard G. Badger, 1920), p. 88.